George A. Cobham, James M. Wells

**Extracts from Letters of Brig. Gen. Cobham**

George A. Cobham, James M. Wells

**Extracts from Letters of Brig. Gen. Cobham**

George A. Cobham, James M. Wells

**Extracts from Letters of Brig. Gen. Cobham**

ISBN/EAN: 9783742808516

Manufactured in Europe, USA, Canada, Australia, Japa

Cover: Foto ©Andreas Hilbeck / pixelio.de

Manufactured and distributed by brebook publishing software (www.brebook.com)

BRIG. GEN. GEO. A COBHAM.

# EXTRACTS

— FROM —

## Letters of Brig. Gen. Cobham,

ALSO, A COMPLETE VINDICATION BY

CAPT. JAMES M. WELLS, 111th Pa. Vols.

## AUTHOR'S PREFACE.

These extracts from the letters of Bigadier General George Ashworth Cobham, Jr., to his mother, sister and brother are respectfully dedicated to his old comrades of the Second Brigade, Second Division, Twelfth Army Corps. Feeling his old comrades would be pleased with these reminiscences of the hard fought fields they have passed over with him, in mutual confidence and emulation. Thinking also that the observations of a participant in the campaign here narrated would be fully as accurate and intertaining as any history yet published, I make no excuse for giving them to the public, and here wish to acknowledge my obligations to Col. W. J. Alexander for his kind assistance and encouragement of my undertaking. The letters to his mother being the most descriptive are mostly selected, but his letters to myself, if they were not largely foreign to the subject, would show more completely the enate nobility of his character.

Very Respectfully yours,<br>
HENRY COBHAM.

*Stonylonesome,*
   *Warren County, Pa.*

Camp Reed, Erie, Pa., Dec. 13, 1861.

DEAR BROTHER:

We are still in Erie, and when we shall leave I do not know. Capt. Sees, an officer of the regular army, arrived in camp yesterday. He was the bearer of dispatches from the Governor to the Colonel, and complimented us very highly on the appearance and drill of our regiment. He says it is the best that has left the state for drill, size of men, and number, the regiment now numbers 983 men. I have had my commission sent to me from the Governor.

Aquia Creek, Va., March 21, 1862.

DEAR MOTHER:

The Second Division of the Twelfth Corps, to which we belong, was received yesterday by Maj. Gen. Hooker, Commander-in-Chief of the Army of the Potomac. After the troops had passed in review and were again formed in line all the commanders of regiments were called to the front and centre and introduced to Gen. Hooker. I had the honor of being introduced to him and shaking hands with him, and of being complimented for the good appearance of the regiment, and told us we should have plenty to do before long.

Harpers Ferry, May 1, 1862.

DEAR MOTHER:

Received orders to march to Strasburg by way of Harpers Ferry, to reinforce Gen. Banks, who was defeated and retreating, pursued by Jackson and Ewell with 20,000 men. In one hour after the receipt of the order we were in march to the railroad. At 6 o'clock next morning we reached Harpers Ferry, where our tents and baggage was left. Two cars with sharpshooters left under command of Col. Schlaudecker, the rest of the regiment under my command pushed on to Winchester. We were the first regiment that arrived, having got ready nearly a day sooner than any other regiment that received orders at the same time. Our orders were to push on as fast as possible to assist Gen. Banks. After going about fifteen miles, we came up with a large number of stragglers from the fight, mostly cavalry soldiers, some of them had thrown away their arms and knapsacks, and some of them had their Sharps' rifles with them. They reported the First Maryland Regiment was cut to pieces, the colonel, major and seven captains killed, and the whole regiment either killed, wounded, or taken prisoners. A short distance on, we were met by two trains containing the First District of Columbia Cavalry, who reported that Banks had retreated back to Martinsburg, and was making a stand, that we were half a day too late too join him, as it was impossible to reach him without attacking the Rebel force. As my orders were to join him, I determined to do so, and gave orders to the men to load their rifles and move on. When we arrived at the place where the two returning trains of soldiers were, we came up with the colonel. After consulting him, and hearing the stories of the retreating soldiers who were all badly frightened, and no two told the same story, with the exception of the retreat of Banks, he agreed with me to move on with our regiment, but the colonel of the returning regiment flatly refused to go back, and as the engineers of the trains were also afraid to go, we could not get past their trains. Meanwhile the 109th Regiment Penn'a. Vol. had arrived, and we gave the men orders to leave the cars to march; but just then a dispatch came from Gen. Saxton to return immediately to Harpers Ferry. Col. Schlaudecker was sent for, to consult with the commander there. Soon the general's aide came up, gave me a sketch of the roads etc., and gave me orders, to go immediately with the 111th to Bolivar Heights and take a position in line of battle, and place the other regiments in line as they arrived, as an immediate attack was expected. I marched to the place indicated, about three miles, and formed in line of battle on the center of the Heights; our center in an orchard on an estate which was deserted, about equal distance from the Potomac on one side, and the Shenandoah on the other. We were soon followed by the following regiments: 109th Penn'a. Vol., 60th N. Y., 1st and 2nd D. C. Vol., 3d and 4th N. Y., 3d Md., 3d Del. and 99th Penn'a. Vol., all infantry; one regiment of cavalry and three batteries of artillery, our line extended from river to river.

HEADQUARTERS 111TH REG'T. PENN'A. VOL.
Camp near Kearnsville Va.
May 7, 1862.

DEAR BROTHER:

Maj. Gen. Seigel is now in command of this division, and we are pushing on as fast as possible to try to overtake the forces of Gens. Jackson and Ewell, they have thirty thousand men, so that when we do overtake them we shall be likely to have a pretty hard fight. I have already been in one, where the 111th Regiment with a few companies of cavalry and two pieces of artillery kept at bay the whole Rebel force from Charleston to Harpers Ferry, and retreated in good order, capturing a large number of their horses and arms, and some prisoners; our loss was one man killed and eight wounded, and two horses killed. The shells and balls flew pretty thick for awhile, the only wonder to me was so few were hurt. A large number of the Rebels were killed by our fire. We had very heavy cannonading for one night and part of the next day, but the Rebels not having any artillery large enough to cope with the 150 and 200 pound Parrot guns mounted on Maryland Heights, they had a large number killed and wounded, so concluded to retreat. Gen. Saxton rode up to our lines and told me to take command of the 111th and march them forward to support the batteries, as he had more confidence in it than any of the others.

Camp in the Woods near Winchester, Va., }
June 5, 1862.

DEAR MOTHER:

Our regiment has been in one fight since we left, succeeded in holding Harpers Ferry and driving back the Confederate forces, although more than four times our number. The 111th was selected to make the first advance, and we have been in advance most of the time since. On Monday evening last we received orders to march immediately to try to overtake Jackson's, Ashley's and Ewell's forces, who were in full retreat toward Winchester, and kept on through the worst rain and mud I ever saw until we came to the Rebel camp, where they had encamped with their whole army, we halted, and occupied the same ground. The camp is the ground on which the battle took place last week between Gen. Banks and the Rebels. There are ten regiments of infantry, one of cavalry and one artillery. Gen. Seigel is now in command.

Camp on Cedar Creek, near Strasburg, Va. }
June 23, 1862.

DEAR BROTHER:

I am now in command of the regiment and have been for some time past. I have also the superintendence of the new bridge at this place. It was put under the charge of the topographical engineers of the regular army, but after he had fussed about it for some time the general sent for me and requested as a favor that I would superintend it, as I was the only practical bridge builder in the division. My rank clears me from being detailed for duties of that kind, but I did accept the office. The whole of the forces are now concentrated near this place and I presume they will all be put under the command of Gen. Fremont, as he is the senior general. There are one-hundred and twenty peices of artillery of the best description attached to this force. The number of men I do not know they are variously estimated at from forty to sixty thousand, but figures are contraband and attack is expected here soon, but with the exception of the occasional shooting of the men on picket duty nothing has taken place yet. The general sent for all the commanding officers of regiments, battalions and batteries to report at nine this morning, he shook hands with me and expressed himself much pleased with the promptness of my regiment, as we were always the first to obey any order and are invariably the first in line and ready to march and is always selected if any regiment is wanted for any special service.

Strasburg, Va., July 2, 1862.

DEAR MOTHER:

We have not had any fighting here yet, there are all kinds of rumors in camp to day from Richmond some stating that it is taken and others that our forces were defeated, it is impossible to tell which is true, but in my opinion we have at least gained nothing and if McClellan is defeated at Richmond in all probability a large part of the Rebel forces will be concentrated to sweep down this valley and try to drive us back to Harpers Ferry and to secure for the Southern army, the large crop of grain now ripe in the valley of Virginia.

Camp at Gaines Cross Roads, Va.<br>July 19, 1862.

DEAR MOTHER:

Precisely at four we left camp at Warrentown, our regiment taking the lead and followed by all the rest with a train of baggage wagons two miles in length, after marching three or four hours we heard distant cannonading, which grew louder as we advanced and continued for some time but the cause of it I do not know.

---

In this interval Col. Cobham was taken sick with typhoid fever and came near dying, and was absent some months from the army.

---

Harpers Ferry, Oct. 23, 1862.

DEAR MOTHER:

I left Baltimore yesterday morning for this place and procured a horse and rode to London Heights, where the regiment is now stationed and found only ninety men fit for duty out of the thousand I left, from here we could see the tents of the Grand Army, the whole ground covered for many miles and in the distance could plainly see the watch fires of the Confederates and their advanced pickets a short distance from ours which plainly indicates that the present quiet state cannot last long.

Harpers Ferry, Oct. 29 1862.

DEAR MOTHER:

The division to which the 111th Regiment is now attached was the first to move. We left London Heights yesterday morning and marched up the valley towards Leesburg, accompanied by the First, Second and Third Brigade of Gen. Burnsides' Corps under the command of Gen. Geary. Our regiment has been assigned to the third Brigade, which is composed of the 111th and 109th Penn'a Regiments and the 78th 137th and 146th New York Regiments and we are attached to Burnsides' Corps. I have been trying to gather together the scattering men belonging to the 111th Regiment who are at the different hospitals and think we will have about four hundred fit for service.

Camp on Bolivar Heights,
Nov. 1, 1862.

DEAR MOTHER:

The forward movement of McClellan's army commenced yesterday morning about 2 o'clock, and from that time the troops have been passing through the town in one unbroken line, regiment after regiment passing along until it was tiresome to see them pass, there were regiments from all the loyal states, among the rest one from California. Many of them were new regiments whose bright new uniforms, arms and accounterments formed a great contrast to the remains of the old regiment, many of which were reduced down to two or three hundred men. Some of their colors were so full of ball holes that there was scarcely enough to hold them together. Our regiment left and went one days march with Gen. Burnside, but were recalled to present camp together with the whole of Gen. Geary's command, I am in command of the regiment, Col. Schlaudecker commanding the brigade.

Bolivar Hights, Nov. 6, 1862.

DEAR MOTHER:

The information you received of my being sick at Baltimore was true, I stayed there for three days and reported to the medical director, who gave me some medicine and told me to report to Gen. Wood and get order for medical treatment, but as I knew if I reported to him I should be under his orders and perhaps sent to command some convalescent camp which would keep me from joining my regiment for some time I preferred to join it at once. I am now well and in command of the regiment in camp at the fort of Bolivar Heights. I have been busy in reorganizing the regiment, and have at last succeeded in getting an order from Gov. Curtin for five hundred and seventy-one men, from the recruits recently drafted from Pennsylvania which is the number required to fill up the regiment to its original number of one thousand men. I sent Lieut. Wells and two non-commissioned officers to Harrisburg last Monday, to take charge of them, and conduct them to camp. I expect they will be here next week. The army has all moved forward, with the exception of Gen. Geary's division, to which we are attached; it is left here for the defense of Harpers Ferry. For the last few days there has been an incessant cannonading heard in the direction of the army, but the cause or the result I do not know. The pickets of the rebels are in sight of our outposts. Yesterday I was appointed Division Field Officer of the Day and was not out of the saddle for twenty-four hours. The duty consists in posting the picket guards and outposts, and visiting them both day and night and instructing the sentinels. The day before yesterday two of the picket guards were captured; two belonged to the 111th. The orders had been not to fire on the enemy's pickets, but yesterday when I took charge of the guard, I ordered them to shoot at every Rebel who came within range of their rifles. Just at dusk the Rebels made another dash on the guards stationed at the same pos twhere the men were captured the night before but were received with a salute from the rifles of the guard and scampered off double quick.

      Headquarters 111th Penn'a. Vol.
      Boliver Heights, Nov. 16, 1862.

DEAR MOTHER:

Col. Schlaudecker has received his papers for an honorable discharge from the regiment, which was drawn up in line and the command formally delivered to me.

      Headquarters 111th Penn'a. Vol.
      Harpers Ferry, Nov. 13, 1862.

DEVR MOTHER:

I suppose you have seen the account of the attack on the Rebels at Charleston by troops from this place,

I was ordered out with regiment at midnight to join the expedition, and when the attack commenced was ordered up to support the batteries with the 111th. As soon as the batteries opened fire the enemy retreated, leaving the camp with their breakfast cooked behind them. I was sent with my regiment and three others from the same brigade to outflank them, but they being cavalry, did not succeed in doing so. All four regiments were under my command. We took a number of horses and beef cattle and did not lose a man.

                Headquarters 111th Penn'a Vol.
                Harpers Ferry, Dec. 7. 1862.

DEAR MOTHER:

I have just returned from an expedition to Winchester and Berrysville. We came up with the enemy's rear guard near Berrysville and some sharp firing took place. I was ordered to the front with my regiment, to support the batteries. I did not lose a man in our regiment, either killed or wounded. Followed on to Winchester and took possession of the town, which was strongly fortified by the Rebels, who were commanded by Gen. A. P. Hill and Gen. Jackson; they thought best to leave. The weather was very cold; on our return it snowed, making it anything but pleasant to sleep on the ground, with the snow blowing over you, as we had to do for six nights, and eat frozen bread and raw pork.

Headquarters 111th Penn'a. Vols.
Camp near Fairfax C. H., Dec. 13th, 1862.

DEAR MOTHER:

Left Harpers Ferry and arrived at this place after four days more marching. We have about five days more marching to reach Fredericksburg. We had to lay our blankets in the snow two nights, and in the mud the other two.

Camp in the Woods, Dec. 19th, 1862.

DEAR MOTHER:

Our orders came unexpectedly for the whole force to march immediately to the assistance of Gen. Burnsides, and for the last eleven days we have been on the march, part of the time by night; also the mud defies description. I never saw anything like it; many fine horses stuck fast, and no effort on the part of the soldiers could extract them and they were left to die where they fell. We crossed Ocoquan river about noon, it is a stream about the size of the Conewango. We had to wade it, which, at this season of the year, is not very pleasant. I was officer of the Grand Guard and had to go the rounds, and bring in all the picket guards from a circle of over five miles, in worse than Egyptian darkness and rain. The cannonading at Fredericksburg, which is in our front, is the heaviest I ever heard. Incessant discharges of the large seige guns making the very earth shake; there being one hundred and fifty at one time by Burnside and probably as many more on the Rebel side. We were again on the march for the scene of action, when orders came to retrace our steps to Fairfax Station to protect the military stores at that place. We have marched now eleven days, without anything to eat from 5 a. m. to 8 p. m., and then only a small piece of salt pork—sometimes not that. As soon as we had stacked arms and a fire was built, I sat down on a log with the regimental order book to write to you. We came up with the enemy's rear guard at Berryville, and some pretty sharp firing took place. I was immediately ordered front with the 111th, to support the batteries. We did not lose a man in our regiment, either killed or wounded. We followed on to Winchester and took possession of the town, strongly fortified. The Rebels under Gen. A. P. Hill and Gen. Jackson, left as we entered; we hurried them by a salute of shell in their rear.

Camp near Fairfax Station, Jan. 1st, 1863.
DEAR BROTHER:

We just returned from another expedition towards Dumfries; we had a fight with some of the Rebel forces on the other side of Ocoquan river, and drove them back. Their loss I do not know, nor do I know the number of killed on our side; those I saw were mostly from the 17th P. V. Our regiment had none killed or wounded. We were immediately ordered to the front to support Knapp's battery, which was then doing all the firing. I had my command of the 111th, and of another regiment, the 109th Penn'a. Vols. also. We started at nine o'clock in the evening of the 28th and marched all night and all the next day, and returned to camp yesterday. Our wagons were ordered back to prevent capture by the enemy's cavalry, and as I had nothing to eat but what was in our regimental wagon, I had the pleasure of going without for two days and a night.

Aquia Creek Landing, Feb. 11th, 1863.

DEAR MOTHER:

Received commission as Colonel of the 111th Regiment of Penn'a Vols., to rank as such from Nov. 7th, 1862. And I have been mustered into the United States service from the same date. My commission was accompanied by a kind letter from Gov. Curtin to me. My promotion has given very general satisfaction in the regiment.

Acquia Creek, Va., Mar. 14th, 1863.

DEAR BROTHER:

The Rebels attacked our camp last night and were repulsed. I think we shall have some hard fighting before long, as we are ordered to be in immediate readiness to move. Our regiment has just received quite a compliment from the Commander-in-Chief of the army. In General Orders No. 18, Army of the Potomac, he says: "It appearing from the Inspector's Report that the 111th Penn'a Vols. has earned high commendation, they are entitled to send one more enlisted man on furlough, for every hundred men reported for duty, and one more commissioned officer than was previously allowed." You may readily believe we are proud of it.

Camp Geary, Va., April 14th, 1863.

DEAR BROTHER:

The whole Army of the Potomac are now on the move, and in all probability before this reaches you, this regiment will have added its feeble mite to the Grand Army of the Potomac, in one of the most desperate struggles that has yet taken place. I have never seen so much preparation for wounded men as is being made. What position we take I do not know, but understand it is to be the right of the advance. It is the determination of all the army to be successful this time; but the victory will be dearly bought.

Headquarters 2d Brig., 2d Div., 12th A. C.
May 8th, 1864.

DEAR SISTER:

I have just returned from the battlefield of Chancellorsville. The fight commenced on the 1st day of May and continued the 1st, 2d, 3d and 4th. The 111th Penn'a Vols. was the first to advance. It is said to be the most desperate battle that has yet taken place. We left camp on the 27th and marched to Kellies Ford, on the Rappahannock, which we reached on the morning of the 29th, at five o'clock. The water was very high and we crossed, without any material opposition from the enemy, on a pontoon bridge; from thence we took the direction of Germania, on the Rapidan river. We arrived at that place about midnight. The advance of the column surprised and captured the Rebel Pioneer Corps, who were building a bridge. We crossed the river at one o'clock a. m., in a severe rain storm, and lay on our arms till daylight, and then after eating a hard cracker soaked with rain for breakfast, we again marched forward. About ten o'clock a. m , the enemy began to open fire on our advancing columns with artillery, from different points which commanded the road, but were soon silenced, and we marched on to the junction of the road from Elys Ford, and one from the United States Ford, on the Rappahannock, where we were joined by the 5th Army Corps, who had surprised one brigade of Rebels, who were digging rifle pits, and routed them, taking a number of prisoners. From here we marched to a small place called Chancellorsville, and filing to the right, for the first time since starting, we laid down on the ground and slept soundly. As the night was dry and warm, and the men had marched with eight days' rations on their back, and sixty rounds of cartridges—we had no wagons or transportation of any kind. The next morning about nine o'clock our scouts reported the enemy to be in force on our front. Our brigade was ordered forward to reconnoitre their position and if possible to ascertain their force. My own regiment, the 111th, being placed in advance. The whole country was a dense forest, so that no view could be had. We deployed as skirmishers and advanced through the woods for about a mile, when our sharpshooters came up with those of the enemy, when the firing commenced. The Rebels also commenced shelling the woods in our front, from batteries which no one could see. We however, moved forward and drove them back till we had accomplished our object of finding out the position of their batteries and the number of their troops. I ordered my men to lay down flat, and the shot and shell all passed over our heads without injuring anyone. As soon as the fire ceased orders came from the general to fall back to our former position, as we had but one brigade and the enemy had about 200,000 men in our front. I was ordered to remain and protect the rear with my regiment, which I did under a heavy fire. As soon as the other regiment had reached their position I was sent out to bring in a section of Knapps' battery, which I did with small loss. One ball cut the hair on the left side of my head, but did me no harm. The Rebels now attacked us with all their force and our batteries having got into position and the troops of our division into line, they met with such a reception as they did not except, they advanced in close column with a loud cheer and a heavy fire from their front lines, supported with batteries, we let them come on until within half rifle shot, when the order was given to fire, both infantry and artillery opened upon them, the fire on both sides was terrible, the grape and canister mowed them down by hundreds, bnt still their officers urged them on, and they moved forward to share the fate of their comrades. At last finding that they had met with a resistance they did not expect they slowly withdrew leaving a very large number of killed and wounded behind them. The night was passed in constructing rifle pits, as we had neither picks nor shovels the men dug up the earth with their bayonets, and threw it up with their tin plates and pieces of wood, which with the help of a few trees cut down made quite a breastwork, which before morning extended eight miles. Saturday morning, the 2nd, the enemy again attacked our line, but were again driven back with great loss, retiring under cover of their artillery. During the day they tried our lines in several places but were driven back with loss every time. About 3 o'clock P. M. the 111th was ordered to take a battery in our front; we moved forward, and as I was leading the regiment, I received a shot in my left breast; it passed through my leather pocketbook which was full of bank bills and papers, a number of photographs, a memorandum book, my field notes, and struck my gold watch which it smashed all to pieces, but with the exception of a severe bruise I escaped unhurt. The Rebels finding themselves unable to force our lines at that point retreated, and for a short time all was still save the groans of the wounded. About sunset the firing again commenced on our right and the whole of Gen. Lee's and Jackson's army made a simultaneous attack on the 11th army corps,—Sigel's old corps—which broke and fell back, letting the enemy into our center, they came on in one solid column into the very center of our position, the artillery was immediately brought to oppose them and some other troops brought forward to assist the 12th corps to drive them back and recover the ground which the Dutch corps had lost. It was now dark, and the scene that took place is beyond my power to describe, every piece of artillery that was possible to get was put in requisition on both sides, the flashes of the cannon and musketry made it almost as light as day and it seemed as if the very earth was rent assunder by the concussion of the guns, and a perfect tornado of shot and shell. grape, canister, rifle and musket balls filled the air, splintering the trees into flagments, tearing up the ground and literally mowing down everything before it. The Rebels advanced through it with undaunted courage determined to take our batteries, which cut them down by the hundred at a time, and the increasing fire of the infantry cut them down as fast as the living could come up to the pile of dead, slowly at last the Rebels gave way and with a cheer our forces drove them over the rifle pits and resumed our former position. Can my dear sister picture to herself such a scene as this battle field presented at this time? A beautiful, still summer's night, and nothing to be heard but the low supressed groans of the wounded who covered the ground in thousands, friend and foe together. I have seen many hard sights but I never wish to see such another as this. In the midst of this scene I laid down on the ground and went to sleep. Both armies slept that night on their arms, but a short distance apart. I awoke next morning at daybreak, it was a beautiful Sunday morning, and got up, my sleep you may imagine was anything but refreshing. I left my regiment for a minute to go to a small spring to get some water, and while washing myself I heard the sharp crack of a rifle close by accompanied by the sharp wistle of the ball followed in rapid sucession by others, and on looking up I saw that the "Grey Backs" were again advancing on our picket line, and the sharp crack of the rifles began to be heard along the whole line.  I immediately rejoined my regiment and in a short time the scene of the previous evening were being again enacted only on a more extensive scale.  If you can picture to yourself a rain of bomb shells and bullets it would be something like it.  One of my officers was struck in the breast with one and instantly killed.  Two soldiers standing near me had the top of their heads shot off, spattering their brains in our faces.  The fire on the position which our regiment new occupied came on us from three sides, front, rear and right flank, we were ordered to fall back, which we did and took position in rear of our artillery, and in connection with the first division of the 12th army corps and again formed line.  The whole army fell back to this point, checked the Rebel forces and held the ground, the fighting on this day was desperate on both sides and the loss very great.  I received another ball through my coat but it did not hurt me.  The fighting here ceased about two o'clock.  The day was exceedingly warm, water scarce and to add to the difficulties we had to encounter the woods which every day caught fire from the shells in all directions.  I have, as you know, seen fire in the woods, but this beat all I ever saw, you can imagine the effect of such stifling heat and smoke on men exhausted with seven days of severe toil; and three of them fighting, with little rest and scant rations. I forgot to mention that I captured during the fighting this day, the battle flag of the 5th Alabama regiment and the captain who carried it. He surrendered his sword and flag to me and I brought them safely with me. The captian's name was Mosely. The flag had the names of eight battles on it. During the night of the 3rd Gen. Kane was compelled to retire, being sick and perfectly exhausted by fatigue and exposure. And I was placed in command of the 2nd Brigade composed of six regiments, we moved down a short distance towards the United States Ford and threw up a new set of breastworks and rifle pits near a small stream called Mine river, we remained there that night and the next day unmolested with the exception of one small attack on our right during the night which was repulsed. About three o'clock in the afternoon it commenced raining and the weather changed from warm to very cold and it rained a perfect deluge, we were without tents of any kind but I heard no complaint from any one. We had by this time exhausted our rations, and it being impossible to furnish them by railroad on account of the failure of Gen. Sedgwick to connect with the army by way of Fredricksburg and the road being so bad that they could not be supplied in time, it was determined to recross the Rappahannock river and take up our former position on the other side of the river. About ten o'clock at night I received notice the army would cross that night and that my brigade would remain till all the rest of the army had crossed and then fall back in as good order as possible and cover the rest of the army. Accordingly at four o'clock in the morning, the others all being gone, I put the column into motion and silently in the dark passed on to the river which we reached at daybreak, I remained on the ground till all had passed, drew in the pickets and followed on in company with Gen. Kane, overtook the brigade and got them all safely over the pontoon bridge without the loss of a man. Gen. Kane was sent in an ambulance to Stafford, from there to Philadelphia. Whatever the newspapers say to the contrary, I know that we had the advantage in every respect and the retreat to the river and crossing was rendered necessary merely on account of want of supplies. We lost twenty-six officers and men killed and wounded in the 111th regiment. I think from what I saw, and I saw the whole fight—being the first regiment to enter it and in command of the last brigade to leave the field — that the loss in killed and wounded on our side must be at least nine thousand men killed and wounded and at least double that on the Rebel side, we took between two and three thousand prisoners. The only relic I brought off the field was a small bible which I picked up and put in my pocket as we came off the field. I can say with the Psalmist of old, I have seen a thousand fall beside me and ten thousand at my right hand. But it has pleased the Almighty to bring me out in safety. I am quite well. The 111th behaved nobly: and have received much praise. In fact the whole of the 12th corps have done all it was possible for men to do. I think Gen. Geary our division commander deserves every praise for his energy, coolness and courage during the whole time his division was engaged. And Major Gen. Slocum, also, the commander of the 12th army corps. I am now in command of the 2nd Brigade, 2nd Division, 12th Army Corps and am ready to move forward again at any time and will try to do my duty wherever I may be placed and under all circumstances.

Camp of the 111th Penna. Vols.<br>May 8th, 1863.

Dear Mother:

I have just returned from the field of battle at Chancellorsville, the fight commenced on the 1st of May and continued four days. Our regiment was the first to advance, and the first man killed was one of the 111th. We lost 26 officers and men. We were under fire all the time, and have seen thousands fall around me. It has pleased the Almighty to spare my life. The 111th behaved nobly. I captured with my own hands the battle flag of the 5th Alabama Regiment with the names of nine battles inscribed on it, and the captain who commanded the color company surrendered me his sword and flag. I am now in command of Gen. Kane's brigade. I cannot tell what was our loss, but think it not less than six thousand and the Rebels ten thousand. The regiment has been highly complimented.

Headquarters 2d Brigade, 2d Div., 12th A. C. }
May 13th, 1863.

DEAR MOTHER:

We have now returned to within one mile of the camp, and think it possible we may remain here a week or two.

Headquarters 2d Brigade, 2d Div., 2d Army Corps, }
Near Aquia Creek, Va., May 22d, 1863.

DEAR MOTHER:

I wrote an account of the late battles, which, although not well written, is true, and may give you some idea of the severity of the fighting. Perhaps the letter may yet reach you with regard to the report in Warren about my watch. It is true. I have sent the remains of it home. The photographs, greenbacks, etc., which Capt. Alexander sent to Younsville were some that were in my pocketbook at the time. Capt. Alexander is one of the officers of the 111th and now acting on the brigade staff as aide de camp, and one I esteem very highly. The shot was a loss of two hundred dollars to me.

NOTE—The letter giving the account of these battles I think never reached his mother. The shot referred to above was a minie ball, which penetrated his pocketbook full of papers and greenbacks and lodged in his watch. We have no account of the many battles that took place from Chancellorsville to June 21st, 1863.

Headquarters 2d Brig., 2d Div., 12th A. C. }
Leesburg, Va., June 21st, 1863.

DEAR MOTHER:

We left camp at Aquia Creek on the 13th inst. and have been pushing forward as fast as possible ever since.

Some of the time we have marched all night as well as day, the object being to intercept Gen. Lee's army and if possible cut off the retreat of that portion of it which has gone into Pennsylvania. I wish they would send me with the infantry and artillery now under my command to follow up the Rebel force that has invaded Pennsylvania. My brigade is now camped on an eminence overlooking the town of Leesburg, and we are throwing up fortifications and digging rifle pits to resist the advance of Gen. Lee's army. I have Knapp's Pennsylvania battery attached to the brigade. The balance of the 12th Army Corps is between us and the Potomac. The people of Harrisburg are a little scared at the few Rebels that have paid them a visit, but they need not be under any apprehension, as their time in Pennsylvania will be short.

Headquarters 2d Brigade, 2d Div., 12th A. C.<br>
June 24th, 1863.

DEAR MOTHER;

We are still located at this place, Fort Beauregard, which is a Rebel earthwork, situate on a commanding eminence overlooking the town of Leesburg. Our brigade is now stationed here with Knapp's Pennsylvania battery. We have repaired the works, and by the addition of the rifle pits, it is now a stong position, and if the Rebels attack us here they will meet with a pretty warm reception. I think we can hold the place against three times our force. It is supposed that the Rebel army will try to force its way through Leesburg to

Edward's Ferry, on the Potomac—which is about three miles from this place—and from there to Washington. The battle field of Ball's Bluff is in sight of this place, about two miles distant. I have been over the ground this morning. It still bears unmistakable evidence of the fight in the bleached bones of horses and the long rows of soldiers graves. It is no wonder to me after seeing the ground that the Union forces were so terribly cut up. Nothing but the grossest ignorance on the part of the commander of that expedition could have induced him to cross the Potomac and attack such a p'ace as this occupied by a far superior force. The outpost pickets of our brigade were attacked this morning by a small Rebel force, we drove them back without loss on our part.

Headquarters of 2d Brigade,<br>Barnesville, Md., June 26th, 1863.

DEAR MOTHER:

I write a few lines in haste to keep you informed of my whereabouts. We left Leesburg this morning at 3 o'clock and crossed the Potomac at Edward's Ferry into Maryland, and marching by way of Poolsville reached this place this evening. It has been a very tiresome march, as it has rained incessantly all day, and we have pushed forward as fast as possible without halting. This move is made to check the advance of Lee's army, as he crossed into Maryland near the Point of Rocks yesterday with about 90,000 men, with the Army of the Potomac after him. I do not have much faith in the

Pennsylvania militia, but hope they will be able to protect Harrisburg.

     Headquarters 2d Brigade,
   Frederick City, Md., June 28th, 1863.

DEAR BROTHER:

Yours of the 21st is just received. I am much pleased to hear from you. With regard to the money from father, you need not mind the two last installments. I will send him a receipt for them as soon as I can get a pen and ink to write one.

    Headquarters 2d Brigade,
 Camp near Littlestown, Pa., July 1st, 1863.

DEAR MOTHER:

The Army of the Potomac is now in Pennsylvania. It has been received in its march through Maryland and Pennsylvania with demonstrations of joy. In every town through which we pass the soldiers are treated in the most hospitable manner, the streets lined with ladies and decorated with flags, and quite different from our experience in Virginia. We encountered no opposition until yesterday afternoon. As we entered Littlestown on the one side the Rebels entered it on the other, a fight of course followed, and the Rebels were driven out and a number of them captured, a few more killed and wounded on each side, I do not know how many. The enemy is in strong force in our front.

Headquarters 2d Brigade,
Battlefield of Gettysburg, Penna., July 4th, 1863.

DEAR BROTHER:

We have just concluded the most severe battle of the war, resulting in a complete victory for the Union forces. The fighting for the past two days has been desperate on both sides. Yesterday at 3 o'clock in the morning our brigade was attacked by Jackson's old troops, and from that time till noon we kept them in check; our men fired two hundred shots each. At noon they charged on us in solid column, and we mowed them down like grass and defeated them entirely. The slaughter has been terrible on both sides; we have not all escaped. You will probably hear of our performance from other sources than myself. It has pleased God to spare me, I was not touched at all. I have, however, to regret the loss of many brave men. All around me as I write the men are burying the dead, the ground is literally covered with them, and the blood is standing in pools all round me, it is truly a sickening sight. I think the Rebels will make another stand before long, between here and the Potomac.

Headquarters 2d Brigade,
Battle Field of Gettysburg, July 5th, 1863.

DEAR MOTHER:

I write a few lines to let you know that I am quite well. We have had the most severe battle of the war at this place. The fight lasted two days and resulted in a complete victory on our side; I passed through it all

without a scratch, although much exposed all the time.
Our brigade was attacked by Stonewall Jackson's old
division, and the fight lasted with them for seven and a
half hours. At the end of that time they charged on us
in a solid column and we drove them back in a perfect
rout. The loss on our side was not very heavy consid-
ering the severity of the fight. Their loss was terrible,
over two thousand dead and wounded were left in front
of our division alone. Gen. Kane returned in an ambulance to his command on the second day of the fight, but
requested me to retain command of the brigade, I had
command all through the fight, and I think you will
hear from other sources that I did my duty. Gen. Kane
leaves again in a few days. We have had nineteen days
of severe marching through dust, rain and mud, night
and day, and marched directly on the battle field and
fought for two days and one night without anything to
eat, or either sleep or rest. I have not had my clothes
off or my boots since we left Leesburg, except once for
a few moments to change my shirt and socks. I carried
one clean shirt on my horse.

> Headquarters 2d Brigade,
> Near Warrenton Junction, Va., July 28th, 1863.

DEAR MOTHER:

The account I saw in the Warren *Mail* of the killed
and wounded of the 111th Regt. at the battle of Gettysburg must have been intended as a burlesque, as I could
hardly imagine anything further from the truth than
that is. It is acknowledged by all here that this brigade

did as hard fighting as any other, and we had to fight ten times our own force. All the attacks made by Ewell's corps were made on us, and the last desperate charge of his whole force was repulsed by the Second Brigade alone; had that succeeded, all was lost. The artillery fire of the Rebels to cover the advance of their infantry, was the most terrible I ever saw—and I have seen a great deal of it—hundreds of round shot and shell struck in every direction each minute. They ripped up the earth, exploded in the air, cut down the trees, and in fact destroyed everything within their range. If you can imagine the shrill screams of hundreds of small steam whistles in the midst of heavy thunder and lightning, then you will form a faint picture of the reality, then you become conscious of the rush of some invisible missle by you, and the man at your side sinks down or is dashed headlong out of the ranks and another steps into his place, perhaps to share the same fate, the next moment. As one sees his former companions and friends fall one after the other he feels a sort of bull dog determination to give as good as he gets, and you can imagine the picture the ground presents after three days of such fighting. Gen. Kane did not remain with the brigade, he came on the second day of the battle and returned immediately after. I understand that his resignation was not accepted and that he has been assigned to duty as commander of the camp for drafted men at Pittsburg, Pa.

Headquarters 2d Brigade,
Near Williamsport, Md., July 10, 1863.

DEAR MOTHER:

The 2d Brigade is drawn up in line of battle here awaiting the commencement of the battle, which is inevitable, as the Rebels are now shelling us, and I write this with the sound of their cannon ringing in my ears, but they have not got our range yet, and before they do I shall have time to finish this letter. Their force is now massed between us and the Potomac, which is about three miles off. Our forces are gradually surrounding them. The river is so high that they cannot cross, and in my opinion it will require all of Lee's generalship to save his army. That he will fight, and fight desperately, there is no doubt of that, he is now giving us ample proof. I suppose you have seen the accounts of the battle of Gettysburg. The Rebel army was defeated with the loss of 40,000 men. Our brigade held the center of the line of the 12th Army Corps. I stationed the men so as to be practically under cover of a ledge of rocks and the sharpshooters behind the trees. They attacked the line immediately in our front; when they charged us in solid column it was the grandest sight I ever saw, I gave orders to cease firing and every man load, and when they were within ten rods we poured in such a fire that they broke and ran in confusion. The slaughter among them was terrible, two thousand killed and wounded being strewed over the ground in front of our division. Our men in that time, seven and a half hours, fired two hundred rounds to the man, the fighting was desperate on all sides; all the army did well. I have not time to write more.

Headquarters 2d Brigade, Aug. 3d, 1863.

DEAR MOTHER:

The pickets of our brigade and the Rebels are now within sight. We advanced to the Rappahannock night before last and laid the pontoon bridge, not, however, without resistance, as our advance was fired on by the Rebels on the opposite bank, they were soon driven back and a part of our force crossed the same night. A sharp fight took place next morning between the cavalry and the Rebels, who were driven back to within a few miles of Culpeper C. H. with considerable loss.

Headquarters 2d Brigade, Sept. 13th, 1863.

DEAR MOHTER:

We are now in position at Racoon Ford, on the river Rapidan. We passed through Culpeper yesterday to this place, which is only a short distance from the battle ground of Cedar Mountain. The enemy are in strong force on the opposite side of the river, and opened a brisk fire of artillery and musketry on us as we advanced. We now hold the line of the Rapidan and have driven the Rebels over.

Headquarters 2d Brig., 2d Div., 12th A. C. }
Sept. 25th, 1863.

DEAR MOTHER:

I write a few lines in haste to let you know that I am on the way to Tennessee. The 12th Army Corps is ordered there.

Headquarters 2d Brig., 2d Div., 12th A. C.
Murfreesboro, Tenn., Oct. 8th, 1863.

DEAR MOTHER:

The journey to Tennessee has been a tiresome one, of 1806 miles from Racoon Ford, on the Rapidan river, Virginia. We have passed through the states of Virginia, Maryland, District of Columbia, Ohio, Indiana, Kentucky and Tennessee. On the first part of the journey we were very kindly received, but more particularly so in passing through the state of Ohio. At every station along the road the ladies had gathered together to welcome the soldiers and supply them with coffee, cakes, pies, biscuits, etc., free of charge, quite a difference from Virginia, where everything of that kind was worth its weight in silver. When you consider that the force that passed through was not less than 20,000 men, you will see it was quite a tax on their generosity. The best reception was from the ladies cf Dayton and Xenia, Ohio, both very pretty places. After passing Indianapolis, Ind., all dem-onstrations of this kind ceased, and the smiling faces of the ladies, their "good-byes" and "God bless you" were seen and heard no more.

Headquarters 2d Brig., 2d Div., 12th A. C.
Nov. 1st, 1863.

DEAR MOTHER:

We have just had another severe engagement with Longstreet's corps of the Rebel army, in which we were completely successful, driving back the enemy with severe loss and opening communication with the army at Chattanooga. Our loss was very heavy, one-fourth of the force engaged in the battle are either killed or wounded. On the evening of Oct. 28th we halted for the night at Wauhatchee, near the base of Lookout Mountain, after three days of severe marching from Bridgeport, Ala., through part of the state of Georgia to this place in Tennessee. My own brigade, two regiments of the 3rd Brigade and one battery of artillery composed the whole of our force engaged, and was under the command of Gen. Geary. A little before midnight on the 28th the enemy attacked our picket line in strong force, I was immediately ordered forward with my brigade to check the advance. I had just time to draw up the brigade in line when the Rebels advanced directly on our front, it was dark, but I could hear them advancing, and ordered the men to lie down. As soon as the advancing lines of the enemy could be seen through the darkness I ordered the men to fire. This was something they did not expect, as they supposed us all to be asleep. They immediately halted and returned the fire, and for three hours we were exposed to a terrible fire. We opened on them with our battery also with terrible effect, the balls flew about our ears like hail in a hail storm. At one time they sent two regiments to turn the right flank of our brigade, and at the same time attacking the left flank of the 3rd Brigade, but I doubled down part of our line and drove them back. Finding it impossible to drive us back and the slaughter in their own ranks so great they gave up the attack and beat a hasty retreat.

Headquarters 2d Brigade, Nov. 15th, 1863.
DEAR BROTHER:

The fighting still goes on here, and it is seldom a day passes without either a fight or a skirmish. In fact, we have been in so many lately for which we have no name, that we call it all "The Grand Skirmish."

Headquarters 2d Brigade, 2d Div., 12th A. C.
Nov. 28th, 1863.
DEAR MOTHER:

Yesterday was Sunday, and I waa sitting in my tent after giving my usual orders, "That everything not absolutely necessary be laid aside, and nothing done that day." The weather was beautifully fine and air mild, more like our September weather in Pennsylvania, and had just sat down to read a new book—"War Pictures from the South," by B. Gastway—with the intention of making myself quite comfortable for the day, and had just got thoroughly interested in the author's fine description of the battle of Manasses, when an orderly rode up and handed me an official letter and immediately galloped of. The letter was from the general, sending his compliments and requesting my immediate presence at headquarters. On my arrival there I saw at once from the number of officers collected there and the orderlies coming and going with dispatches that as they say here, something was up. The general shook hands with me and said: "Colonel, we are called on once more to victory and strike a decisive blow, and with the help of Almighty God I trust we shall succeed." And he gave me a detailed account of the plan of operations intended and of the part assigned to myself and the troops that would be under my command and ordered to report to me, with the usual caution, "To keep the information to myself." I could not help contrasting this with similar meetings previous to the battles of Chancellorsville, Gettysburg and other occasions of a similar kind, and wondering whose place would be vacant next time, as all never meet again, some familiar face is always absent. I returned to my quarters, where the shrill notes of the bugle, sounding the officers call, soon assembled my own brigade officers, and every preparation was made to carry out our part of the movement, which was to take place at daylight next morning. Arms were inspected and rations and sixty rounds of ammunition were issued to each man. The regiments moved quickly to their positions, artillery posted and everything in readiness to give the Rebels a grand salute, but at midnight orders came postponing the attack.

    Headquarters 2d Brig,, 2d Div., 12th A. C. }
      Ringold, Ga., Nov. 29th, 1863.    }

DEAR MOTHER:

  I suppose you have already seen in the papers accounts of the battles of Lookout Mountain, Mission Ridge and Ringold, and will no doubt be anxious on my account. I take the first opportunity to write and tell you that I have passed through all those fights unhurt and quite well. At the storming of Lookout Mouutain my brigade was selected to take the advance and the right of the front of battle, and it was our brigade which first planted their colors on top. The fighting was desperate, but we charged bayonets on the enemy and drove them out of their fortifications and took more prisoners than we had men engaged. The defeat of the Rebels was complete, and they lost the most formidable stronghold in the South. I have seen many mountains, but I never saw such a one as Lookout. Its sides are very steep and rocky and almost impossible to climb at all, and at the top a perpendicular ledge of rock, which we had to climb with scaling ladders.

On the next morning after the battle of Lookout Mountain General Sherman attacked the Rebels on Mission Ridge, and the result was a general engagement of the most desperate description along the whole line— Hooker's force, to which we belong—was immediately put in motion to turn the right flank of Bragg's army, which we succeeded in doing, and by sundown the whole of the Rebel force was utterly routed. Prisoners were taken by thousands, whole brigades being captured at once, both officers and men. Gen. Breckenridge's son was captured, he was aide to his father, and the general came very near accompanying his son to Washington. A very large number of cannon were captured also, the ground was covered for a long distance with arms and accourtrements which the Rebels threw away. We camped in the Rebel camp on Mission Ridge that night and the next morning we started again in pursuit and marched until midnight, when the brigade in advance of me came up with their rear guard, attacked it and captured their battery and a number of prisoners. We then lay down on the ground and waited for day, and started again without breakfast or supper either, as we had only one day's rations when we started and none could follow us, as the bridges were all destroyed and we had to make foot bridges for the men and swam our horses over. About ten o'clock the next day we got to Ringold, where there is a large chain of mountains, with a gap or pass, through which the railroad to Atlanta passes, here the Rebels made a desperate stand. Their artillery was posted in the gap and their infantry drawn up on the top of the mountains on each side, and the whole side of the hill, which is covered with a heavy growth of oak timber, was full of sharpshooters. As soon as the head of the column got to the town the enemy opened fire on us with both cannon and rifles. As we marched down the main street of the town the minie balls were flying around in all directions. The women were leaving the few houses that were then inhabited in a hurry, with the comforting reflection that it was their own brothers, fathers and husbands that were firing on them. We paid no attention whatever to the fire, but pushed on till we came to the railroad depot; from here we had to cross a field to reach a slight elevation near the foot of the hill and in front of the enemy's center, under a most terrible fire of musketry and artillery, the whole air was shrieking with balls and shells. I jumped off my horse and ordered the brigade forward double quick, and took the lead myself in advance of the men, and thus crossed one of the hottest places I have ever seen. I got two balls through my overcoat in the operation, but neither of them touched my body. As soon as we reached the point I ordered the men to lie down under cover of the little rise of ground, and all the fire of the enemy enemy could not dislodge us, as their balls all flew over our heads quite harmless, whilst ours were quite the reverse to them. After three hours' fighting their flank was turned by the 1st Brigade, and they took to their heels and we remained in undisturbed possession of all the country, from Lookout Mountain to Ringold, 40 miles. Our brigade is now here and one regiment, the 111th, guarding the gap. It is not intended to pursue the enemy any further by this route. In fact, our men are tired out and cannot go any further without supplies.

Headquarters 2d Brigade, 2d Div., 12th A. C.
Bridgeport, Tenn., Dec. 9th, 1863.

DEAR MOTHER:

We are not now annoyed with Rebel pickets and can now sleep all night without any shells coming screaming through the camp. There is not a Rebel within thirty miles of us, and the ground that a few weeks ago was covered with their camps, as far as the eye could reach, is vacant now, not a tent to be seen. The battles of Lookout Mountain, Mission Ridge and Ringold have been the most serious reverses the Rebels have met during the war, as they have lost very heavily in killed, wounded and prisoners and 64 pieces of artillery, including the two celebrated cannon, named Lidia Breckenridge and Lady Buckner, named after the wives of two of their generals. We destroyed the Memphis and Charleston Railroad for many miles. When the order to fall back was given I was in the advanced outpost. War is a stern reality, and none but those who witness it can form an idea of its horrors.

Headquarters 2d Brig., 2d Div., 12th A. C.<br>
Bridgeport, Tenn., Jan. 11th, 1864.

DEAR MOTHER:

I write a few lines in haste to inform you of my safe arrival at this place on the 7th inst., the last day of my leave, so that I was back in time. You will, I know, be pleased to hear that I am again coming home, and shall be there almost as soon as this reaches you on another leave of thirty days, so that this time I shall have the pleasure of making you a long visit at Cobham Park. The whole of my brigade have reinlisted and the last regiment of the brigade goes home to Philadelphia in a few days, and myself and staff will accompany it to that city, where brigade headquarters will be located until the return of the regiments.

Headquarters 2d Brig., 2d Div., 12th A. C.<br>
Bridgeport, Tenn., Jan. 19th, 1864.

DEAR MOTHER:

I have the recommendations of Gens. Kane, Geary, Slocum and Hooker, which is quite an honor, if I get nothing more. Gen. Geary has written me a recommendation for promotion. Maj. Gen. Hooker also gave me a recommendation to the Secretary of War during my absence. I also received a letter from Maj. Gen. Slocum, commanding 12th Army Corps, a few days ago, saying that he had written a letter of recommendation for my promotion to the Secretary of War.

Headquarters 2d Brig., 2d Div., 12th A. C.<br>Bridgeport Tenn., March 10th 1864.

DEAR MOTHER:

I arrived at this place yesterday with my regiment, and we have gone into camp here. I was kindly received by the general and his staff on my arrival, and all of us were warmly welcomed back by the members of our old division. I was immediately reinstated in my former position, and am now in command of the 2d Brigade, to which two more regiments are to be added. How long I shall remain in command I do not know, but presume until some new general is appointed.

Headquarters 2d Brig., 2d Div., 12th A. C.<br>April 12th, 1864.

DEAR MOTHER:

On my arrival here I found my things all safe and my two horses also safe, in good condition and looking very well. My old friend, Col. French, had taken charge of them, and I am indebted to him for having taken such good care of my horses and baggage. It is very lonely here, and it will take some time to become accustomed to camp life again. I shall be glad when the war is over, to enjoy once more the comforts of civilized life. There is some prospect of the 12th Army Corps being sent to the Army of the Potomac, which I hope may be the case, we shall not be so far out of the world then as we are now.

Headquarters 2d Brig., 2d Div., 12th A. C.
April 14th, 1864.

DEAR MOTHER:

I presume you will have seen by the newspapers that the 11th and 12th Army Corps have been consolidated and are to form one corps under Gen. Hooker, and both the former corps commanders are assigned to other commands. Maj. Gen. Slocum is now ordered to the command of Vicksburg, and will leave immediately for that place. He called on me yesterday to bid me "good bye" and very kindly volunteered his services in any way that would lead to my advancement. I have never parted with an officer whose loss I regretted as much as I do that of Gen. Slocum. I have commanded a brigade in his corps during every battle in which the corps has been engaged since the battle of Antietam, and regret not only his loss, but the consolidation of the 12th Corps, with which I have been so long identified. I do not know how the new corps will be organized or who will command divisions or brigades.

Headquarters 2d Brig., 2d Div., 12th A. C.
Bridgeport, Tenn., April 20th, 1864.

DEAR MOTHER:

I have just seen Gen. Hooker's official report of the battles of Lookout Mountain, Mission Ridge and

Ringold. It is published in the Cincinnati *Commercial* of April 14th. In some places where my name is mentioned it is spelled right and in some I am flourishing under the name of Coburn. As the consolidation of the 12th Corps breaks up my brigade with the rest, I go back to the command of my regiment. I am assigned to duty in the 3d Brig., 2d Div., 20th Army Corps. Although the breaking of any organization which has passed together through so many hard marches and desperate battles, as has been the case with my brigade, must necessarily be attended with much regret by all, still I have the consolation of knowing that I leave command of this brigade to the sincere regret of every member, both officers and men composing it, and the men who never murmured when ordered into the hottest fire of Gettysburg or Lookout Mountain, where almost certain death stared them in the face, obey with great reluctance an order which simply assigns them to another brigade commander. For my own part, although I regret to part with many of my old companions in arms, I am determined to do my duty wherever I am placed. I know as well as anyone that it is no compliment to me to be sent back to my regiment after being in command of a brigade for over a year, having joined it in April, 1863, and I am proud to say it has won a reputation second to none in the army, but I am the only one who does not complain.

Headquarters 111th Penn'a Vet. Vol., }
Bridgeport, Tenn., April 23, 1864. }

DEAR SISTER:

Letter writing has got to be quite a bore to me, as I have got to answer all the letters of almost every man, woman and child who happens to have husband, brother, father, cousin or sweetheart in the army serving under my command. They all think I must be well posted in their affairs, and that nobody could have the toothache or nosebleed without my knowing it, and write and inquire how Mr. Jones or Mr. Smith is and where they are. They little imagine the impossibility of finding them, unless rank, regiment and company are stated. In one instance I received a letter from a little girl of eight years old inquiring of me where her dear papa was, as she had not heard of him for a month. After considerable difficulty I found her father, he was in the general hospital, and found out from him where his little daughter lived, as she had forgotten to tell that in her letter, supposing I knew all about it. I wrote and told her her father was well. I always answer letters of this kind. I was honored with a very fine serenade the last night of my stay in the capacity of brigade commander. It was a beautiful moonlight night, and I was sitting in my tent writing some letters, when all at once bands struck up in front of my quarters, playing the perhaps appropriate piece, "We Shall Meet, but we Shall Miss Him," a glee club singing the air and the bands playing the accompaniment. In my going out I found almost all the officers of my old brigade and a number of others from other regiments and the artillery officers of the battery. They had collected the musicians of the different regimental bands, and had come to bid me a parting serenade. The evening passed very pleasantly, and if I had as large a place as stepfather's new house to receive them all in I would have had quite a house full. It was about 1 o'clock when they left, all of them leaving with the kindest expressions of regard. This, my dear sister, is one of those pleasant scenes once in a soldier's life, which repays him for many dangers, hardships and privations, and the recollection of which cheer up and enliven one during many dull and lonely hours.

Headquarters 111th Penn'a Vol., }
Near Dalton, Ga.. May 9th, 1864. }

DEAR MOTHER:

I write this to let you know that I am safe and well. We had a hard fight yesterday and there will be another to-day. Our division lost quite heavily in officers and men. We are now four miles from Dalton and advancing rapidly on that place. The enemy is in strong force there.

Headquarters 111th Penn'a Vol., }
Near Dalton, Ga., May 12th, 1864. }

DEAR MOTHER:

There has been constant fighting for some days, but it has been confined to not more than one division at a time, for the purpose of securing the different gaps in the mountains held by the Rebels. The loss on both sides has been heavy, but nothing to what it likely will be in the assault that must soon take place. The loss in killed and wounded in this division so far is 359, including two colonels and a number of other officers. I think there is little doubt of the immediate capture of Dalton. The 16th Army Corps has got possession of the railroad from Dalton to Atlanta and destoyed it, and are now moving up in the rear of the Rebel army at Dalton, whilst we attack them in front. As this railroad is their main line of communication for supplies, the loss of it to the Rebel army is very great.

Headquarters 111th Penn'a Vol.,
Ressaca, Ga., May 14th, 1864.

DEAR MOTHER:

We had a severe battle yesterday. Dalton is in possession of our troops. The Rebels are falling back on Atlanta. The fighting is still going on and we are pursuing the Rebels, who will no doubt make another stand at some point. I am safe and well so far; I do not know the number of killed and wounded. I have no time to write more, as we go into the fight.

Headquarters 111th Penn'a Vol.,
Pine Chapple, Ga., May 17th, 1864.

DEAR MOTHER:

I write again to let you know that I am still safe and quite well. I have passed through the fighting so far unhurt; we have had terrible fighting for the last three days, but we have beaten the Rebels at every point. They are falling back on Atlanta and we are in full pursuit.  At the battle of Ressaca, on the 15th, I captured a Rebel battery of four 12-pounders, and brought the guns off with my regiment, in spite of all efforts of the Rebels to prevent it.  Our loss was heavy.  We took their fort also, it being between our lines and the enemy's, who made most desperate efforts to save their guns.  We had no cover of any kind, as the opening or entrance to the battery faced to and connected with the Rebel works, so I ordered the men to lie down and fire, and no Rebel dared to lift his head above their breastworks, if he did he never lived to tell of it, no man could stay in the battery and live, so at night, having large reinforcements sent me, I set the pioneers to work, under cover of our rifles, and dug away the face of the battery on our side and drew out the guns, four brass 12-pounders, with the limbers, caissons and ammunition.

I am now in command of a brigade again and have seven regiments, the 111th P. V., 29th P. V., 60th N. Y. V., 78th, 102d, 149th and 137th N. Y. V.  The fighting lasted three days continuously, and there has been continued skirmishing.  We expect to overtake the retreating Rebel army to-day.  We are in advance of the whole army and pushing forward as fast as possible.

Camp in the Field, near Kingston, Ga.,
May 20th, 1864.

DEAR BROTHER:

The fighting at the battle of Ressaca lasted three days, and was most desperate on both sides, and resulted in the total rout of the Rebel army.  I was selected by

Gen. Hooker to lead the charge on the Rebel batteries, and succeeded in taking the position in the forenoon and holding it until night and brought off the guns of their battery as trophies. After I had charged upon and taken the fort with my own regiment, Gen. Hooker placed me in command of all the troops sent up to hold the position. I can only describe the fire we received by saying it was terrible. Grape, cannister and rifle balls literally filled the air, I was not touched at all. All, however, were not so fortunate, as blue and gray coats literally covered the ground. How I escaped I do not know, as I had my full uniform on and took the lead. After the battle was over the general requested me not to wear my star bagde, as it was only running an extra risk, so I now wear it on my vest. The Rebels have been driven from every position so far, Tunnel Hill, Buzzard Roost, Mill Creek Gap, Dalton, Ressaca and Kingston. We have had a most severe campaign, constant marching and fighting, day and night, under a sun hot enough to roast eggs. We expect the Rebels to make a desperate stand at Altoona and again at Atlanta. I have not had my clothes or boots off for the last ten days, except to wash and sleep on the ground.

Camp in the Field, near Cassville, Ga.,<br>May 22d, 1864.

DEAR MOTHER:

I believe I told you in my last letter that I was again in command of a brigade, how long I shall continue to do so I do not know. We have had very hard fighting, but have been successful so far, and we are following the retreating Rebels rapidly. We expect them to make another determined stand near Otowah to-morrow or next day; it is a strong position, but I think we can take it. The Rebels are about 80,000 strong.

Camp in the Field, near Dallas, Ga.,
May 24th, 1864.

DEAR MOTHER:

I write you a few lines from the battlefield this evening to let you know that I am safe and quite well. We have had another severe battle here. The fighting lasted two days, commencing at 10 a. m. yesterday and continued until dusk this evening. We have driven the Rebels from their position and back about five miles with severe loss. Our loss was also heavy. My brigade was engaged during both days' fighting, and has suffered severely in killed and wounded. Every man from Warren in the 111th Regiment, excepting myself, is either killed or wounded. Although I was fully exposed on horseback during the whole fight, I was not touched at all. We are now only 35 miles from Atlanta, and hope to reach that place in three days more, but I think we shall have some hard fighting yet before we reach it. I have seen some desperate and bloody scenes, such as I do not wish to see again.

On the Battlefield, near Dallas,
May 29th, 1864.

DEAR MOTHER:

As I presume you will be anxious on my account, I sit down to write again, to let you know that I am still safe and well. The fighting is still going on all around, and the balls, shells and grape shot are flying past thickly as I write this. This makes the fifth day that my brigade has been constantly engaged in fighting without cessation or rest. The battle commenced on the 25th inst. at 10 a. m. and continued on the 26th, 27th, 28th and 29th, and up to this time is still going on. Yesterday the enemy made a determined charge on my brigade under cover of a most severe artillery fire, but we repulsed them with heavy loss. We also drove their gunners from their guns and held their battery all day and the sharpshooters of my brigade still hold them, so that no man can load the cannon. The entire battle ground is thick woods and the lines of both armies are now entrenched and are only about 20 rods apart. The Rebel works are strong, but I expect an attempt will be made to carry them by assault in front and in flank at the same time. We occupy the front. Our division has lost over 1,000 men in killed and wounded in the last two weeks. The 111th, which is in this brigade, has also lost heavily. All in it from Warren are killed or wounded. The Rebels have their whole army here, and our strength is about equal. Our army has been successful thus far. I think the enemy intend to make this their last and most desperate stand.

    Headquarters 3d Brig., 2d Div., 20th A. C. }
     Near Altoona, Ga., June 2d, 1864.   }
DEAR MOTHER:

  We have just passed through one of the hardest times it has been my fortune to witness since I have been in the service. Our Corps—the 20th—attacked the enemy on the 25th, and it has been constant fighting from that time until last night. We have been under fire constantly day and night for eight days, and am happy to inform you that I am still spared to fight again, being unhurt and quite well. I have not been off duty a minute since I left home. We have been successful thus far and have driven the enemy steadily back, but we shall have hard fighting yet. We are about 30 miles from Atlanta. The 111th has lost 94 killed and wounded. My brigade loss is 400; the 2d Division 1175. I am sorry to part with so many brave men as we have lost in this campaign. Warren has suffered severely, but their friends will have the consolation of knowing that they fell whilst nobly doing their duty. I got through the kindness of the Hon. Morrow B. Lowery, of Erie, a recommendation to the Secretary of War for promotion, signed by nearly all the members of the Pennsylvania Senate and House of Representatives, but I feel about as proud of my "Old Eagles," who have been through so much fire, as I should be of a star. Maj. Gen. Hooker paid me a visit yesterday and stayed about an hour. He is well pleased with our progress thus far. This makes thirty-one days we have been constantly on the march or fighting, and during that time I have not had my clothes or boots off, except to wash and sleep on the ground, when I can get time to sleep.

Headquarters 3d Brig., 2d Div., 20th A. C. }
Camp near Kenesaw Mountain, June 4th, 1864. }

DEAR MOTHER:

I take advantage of the departure of Capt. Green, late of my brigade staff, who leaves this morning for Philadelphia, to write and let you know that I am still alive and well. There it every prospect of more hard fighting here very soon, as the Rebels hold a very strong position on our front, and from where I am writing I can see them in plain sight on the hills planting their batteries less than half a mile distant.

Headquarters 3d Brig., 2d Div., 20th A. C. }
Ackworth, Ga., June 5th, 1864. }

DEAR MOTHER:

The fighting is now over for a few days. We have driven the Rebels from all their positions, and they are again falling back. Our troops now hold Altoona, Ackworth and will occupy Marietta this morning. It is 20 miles from Atlanta. I presume the Rebels will make one more stand before reaching Atlanta, perhaps at the river, eight miles from that point. We now have uninterrupted railroad communication here as soon as the bridge is rebuilt, which will be done in a day or two.

Camp in the Woods, near Marietta, Ga., }
June 9th, 1864. }

DEAR MOTHER:

I am busy making out my official reports of the late battles and getting my command in readiness for another advance on the enemy, as we are to advance at daybreak in the morning.

Headquarters 111th Penn'a Vol.,
Near Marietta, Ga., June 17th, 1864, 5 a. m.

DEAR MOTHER:

Our Corps—the 20th—has had another severe engagement with the Rebels. At noon of the 15th inst. we attacked them and a severe fight took place, which lasted till after dark. We drove them steadily back for near two miles, taking their works as we advanced and driving them into their rear line of works, which was very strong, with sharp stakes driven in front at an angle of 15°, very sharp and difficult to pass. We hold the position, planted batteries and built breastworks also, under fire. The fighting continued between our batteries and sharpshooters and those of the enemy all day yesterday and until 1 a. m. this morning, and by 4 o'clock the Johnnie Rebs had made a masterly advance on Atlanta by the rear rank, and I now write sitting on their breastworks to the music of our cannon, which are thundering on their rear, admonishing them to hurry up. They will stand again at the river, if not before. This kind of work is very tiresome, and all feel one day older than we did yesterday at this time, but we intend to follow them up, as they say in Georgia "Right Sharp." I do not know our exact loss, but think it will not exceed 15 or 20 in the 111th and 125 in the brigade. It has pleased the Almighty to bring me through this fight unhurt and quite well.

Headquarters 111th Penn'a Vol.,
June 20th, 1864.

DEAR MOHTER:

I wrote to you on the 17th, immediately after our fighting of the 15th and 16th, and on the morning of the 18th we again drove the Rebels from their breastworks, and yesterday, the 19th, we again attacked them with same result. Our loss in these last engagements I do not think very large, but when you take it into consideration that we have a fight or skirmish every day, it will be easy to see that the members of my regiment are decreasing very fast. I left Bridgeport on the 3d of May with an effective force of 573 officers and men for duty, and at roll call this morning they numbered all told, officers and men, 250. Of the number lost 130 have been killed or wounded in battle, the rest sent to the rear as sick and worn out.

Headquarters 111th Penn'a Vol.,
June 23th, 1864.

DEAR MOTHER:

I write to let you know we have had another fight, yesterday and this morning. We attacked the Rebel breastworks and drove them out again. Our loss was only two officers and 10 men in the 111th. The Rebel loss was very heavy. We have gained a very important position. I was not hurt, and am as usual, quite well. Please excuse this poor letter, it is the best I can do this time.

Headquarters 111th Penn'a Vol., }
Millgrove, Ga., July 4th, 1864.

DEAR MOTHER:

Yesterday morning before daylight the Rebels again retreated from their breastworks, where they have held out so long, and where there has been so much hard fighting. They had four lines of strong earthworks. I think they are the strongest I ever saw, but at last we outflanked them, and they had to make another hasty retreat. I happened to be General Officer of the Day, and in charge of all the pickets and skirmishers of the division, and about midnight I received notice from headquarters that it was expected the enemy would evacuate their works that night, as two corps of our army were then on their left flank, and they would be attacked on that flank. Our position was near the center of their line and so close to it that I could throw a stone into their first line of works. I immediately visited every picket post and ordered our men to cease firing and not to return the Rebel fire, as I wished to find out if possible if they were moving to the rear. You can readily imagine that this sort of duty is not very pleasant. At the least mistake in going from one post to another, through the woods and in the dark—to carry a light would be certain death—would bring you into the enemy's lines, and a constant fire is kept up on every thing seen or heard, and the whistle of minie balls is constantly heard. Between 1 and 2 o'clock the fire of the Rebel pickets ceased, and with the exception of an occasional shot along the line—which extended for several miles—all was still. As soon as daylight came sufficient to see to move, I ordered the whole line of skirmishers forward, going myself in command of them. It was a time of fearful suspense to all of us, the few moments occupied in passing from our own line of works to the first line of the enemy's, as we did not of course know whether we should occupy the works without opposition, or whether we should be fired on and driven dack by the Rebels, but we met with no opposition, all was still and we entered their first line of works without difficulty. I immediately sent a dispatch to the general informing him of the fact. When I received orders to push the skirmishers forward and ascertain if possible the movements of the enemy, I moved the line forward at once and passed over three more lines of the strongest kind of breastworks, on the side of the hill, one above the other. The upper one was a work of the stronges kind, with strong redouts for cannon at intervals along the whole line, and sharp pointed stakes driven in the front, so as to render it almost impossible to get into it even when unoccupied. It would have cost us thousands of lives to have taken their works by assault in front. On entering the upper line of works I found every indication of a hasty retreat of its former defenders. The works bore strong indications of heavy loss on the part of the Rebels in wounded, and I saw a large number of fresh graves along the line. One Johnnie Reb who had not been quick enough with his breakfast, we captured. From him I learned that the Rebel army commenced moving about midnight on the right, and that all were ordered to fall back as soon as possible, but he did not know where they were ordered to. I ordered my line of skirmishers forward towards the railroad, four miles distant, and after going rapidly about half a mile I came up with the rear guard of Cheatham's division of Gen. Aood's corps, composed mostly of cavalry, who were hurrying up all before them. I immediately fired into them, which compliment they returned and hurried off. We followed up as rapidly as possible in skirmish order, sheltering my men from their fire and firing on them at every opportunity and taking some of them prisoners at almost every step. We annoyed them much the same as a swarm of bees would a mad bull. In this way the fight continued until we reached the railroad, where the Rebels made a stand and brought their artillery to the rear, supported by a strong infantry force, and opened a fire of musketry and artillery on us with shell and grape and canister. Being determined not to give it up, I posted my men behind trees, stumps, etc., and returned their fire with impunity, as they were exposed to sight and could not see one of our men. Gen. Geary hearing the artillery, immediately sent one section of Knapp's battery to our assistance, and as soon as that opened fire the enemy immediately retreated, leaving us in possession of the field. I received orders to withdraw my skirmishers, as our division was ordered to Millgrove. In this affair we captured 150 Rebel prisoners and brought them back with us. Among those killed was one colonel of a Georgia regiment. The Rebels lost very heavily, whilst our loss was very trifling, none killed and but few wounded. I received the compliments of some Reb in the shape of a minie ball through my coat, on the right side, but it did not touch my body, but made a job for the tailor, instead of the doctor. A large number of prisoners were taken to-day, and I think Sherman will order an attack this evening or in the morning on the Rebel lines, as they are in plain sight of us again. The movements of this army has been very successful, and although the whole army has not been engaged at one time, still the fighting has been as severe for those that were engaged as any there has been in the Army of the Potomac.

Headquarters 111th Penn'a Vet. Vol.,  
Near Quring's Station, Ga., July 8th, 1864.

DEAR BROTHER:

Judging from the few newspapers that I see I think you do not hear much of the operations of this army. The movements of the Army of the Potomac has engrossed the attention of all the Northern and Eastern papers. One reason of this is that Gen. Sherman has banished all regular newspaper correspondents from the army. All of them have to go to Virginia or remain out of employment. The campaign here has presented many difficulties and hardships, of which the Potomac army knows nothing. Sherman's army numbers to-day not far from one hundred and twenty thousand men. There has been no general engagement yet where all this force has been engaged at one time, as has been the case with our old comrades in Virginia. The fighting here has generally been confined to a portion of the army at a time, and has in every instance been assaults upon formidable positions strongly fortified. We are now far from our base of supplies—about two hundred and fifty miles—and the whole distance through the enemy's country. We have been for over two months constantly on the march or fighting, and have driven the enemy and compelled them to leave every position they have taken, extending over one hundred miles. The fortifications from which they have been driven were considered by them as impregnable. They were not works hastily constructed by the soldiers—as was the case with us—but have occupied the labor of thousands of black and white, under the direction and supervision of experienced engineer officers, and have been finished long since in anticipation of a repulse. It is difficult to conceive of stronger positions than some of these we have taken, and we have more of them to take yet. Our corps—the 20th—has certainly done more and harder fighting than any other corps in the army, and Hooker's men are well known for their fighting qualities. The corps has lost one-half its number since it left Bridgeport on the 3d of May last. I have never seen more desperate and bloody fighting than I have seen in Georgia. I have seen hundreds, yes thousands fall in but a few minutes, and yet seen even the least mention of it in the papers, other than Sherman's laconic dispatches to Secretary Stanton of his having made an assault at such a time and place. It is very different with the Army of the Potomac. There every battle, skirmish or movement of any kind is fully described in all the papers, with all the incidents and details, while we look in vain for any account of our movements.

Headquarters 111th Penn'a Vet. Vols.,
Nickajack Creek, Ga., July 6th, 1864.

DEAR MOTHER:

We have come up with the Rebel army in a strong position, which they have had fortified for some time past ready to fall back to. Our artillery are now shelling their works and they will be driven out of them before long. A large number of the Rebels have been taken prisoners in the last few days. It is only nine miles from here to Atlanta, and this morning I had the pleasure of seeing the spires of the churches and some of the buildings in the town for the first time, so you see we are at least in sight of the objective point of this campaign. It may be weeks before we get possession of the place, but it is now only a question of time. I think the result is certain and hope we shall have an opportunity to rest them.

> How soon he was to take a long last rest,
> The rest that he had needed for so long;
> It fell soon, and was it welcome too?
> We have no means to judge, but deem it was
> A life of trouble from the very first.

Cared more for others than he did for self,
Self-sacrifice impress'd on all his deeds;
We feel his gentle spirit did not blend
With the sad scenes of strife in which he mix'd.
His heart, it was at variance with strife,
In other things was gentleness itself;
Forbearent even to the greatest wrong
That man can meet with from his fellow men,
Ingratitude and treachery, 'tis said,
And truly—as we have the means to know—
'Twas only duty call'd him to the field,
And duty kept him foremost to the last.
As Nelson, and as other gentle hearts,
Exemplar of the motto of his race:
"Spirit is Noble," as it was in him,
Under which renown has been won before
By his progenitors, at Smithfield one,
In the crusades, as in intestine war
'Twixt rival Roses, one on Basworth field
At Paris, with the Duke of Burgundy,
At Calias, too, one saved the English cause,
Not one of whom was braver than himself;
And few there be as pure, as kind, as good,
And died a hero, in his country's cause,
To the regret of comrades of all grades,
With the respect of all his fellow men;
The country, too, express'd its gratitude,
By gift of stars, he had so nobly earn'd,
In which the House and Senate both concur'd,
But all too late to gladden his sad life,
He fell, not knowing all the praise he won.

Headquarters 111th Penn'a Vet. Vol.,
Chatteroochie River, Ga., July 13th, 1864.

DEAR MOTHER:

We have had no fighting for the last few days, and I am of the opinion that we shall have an opportunity to rest for a short time. The enemy have been driven into their works around Atlanta, and our troops are now but a short distance from it. The campaign thus far has been a complete success. What the next move will be I do not know. All the troops have gone into camp and we are enjoying the first rest we have had for two months. I have sent back for my baggage, and hope soon to have my clothes and writing desk with me again for a short time at least. I have never before been so badly off for all the comforts of life as I have been on this campaign. All the clothes I have been able to carry with me was what I could put into the small round valise at the back of my saddle, namely, one shirt, two pairs of socks, which with some soap, a couple of towels and a tooth brush completed my outfit. I think you must be tired of reading the same old story of fighting, skirmishing, marches, etc., but that has been the order of the day with us, and I see but little else. I shall be very glad when I can write and say that the last battle has been fought and that the war is over. I was visited the other day by two officers who belonged in the Second Brigade of the 12th Army Corps during all the time that I commanded it—over a year. They handed me a paper and requested me to read it, which I did, and you may imagine I was somewhat surprised to find that it was a request to the Secretary of War for Col. Cobham to be promoted to the rank of Brigadier General of Volunteers, and signed by every one of the surviving officers of the old brigade. It happened that all the regiments that formerly composed it were camped near together and the officers of the 29th Penn'a Vols.—which are from Philadelphia—drew up the paper and all the other officers of the regiment signed it, entirely unknown to me. They told me they were going to send it on by one of the officers who was going home after having presented it to some others for signature. Although recommendations are no use now-a-days, it is certainly very gratifying to know that those who have served with me so long and who have risked their lives so often under my command, should have such a good opinion of me. I feel much obliged to them for the compliment, but as for the promotion, I care but little about it. I think perhaps it is better to be a good colonel than a poor general. We have plenty of the latter now.

Headquarters 111th Penn'a Vet. Vol.,<br>Near Atlanta, Ga., July 11th, 1864.

DEAR BROTHER:

I am pleased to hear that you have paid my taxes. They do not amount to as much as I supposed. You will, of course, pay them out of my money. I had expected to have been paid by this time, but there is no prospect of it until this campaign is over. As soon as I receive my pay I will forward the money to you by express. Since I wrote last to you the enemy have been compelled to retreat again and leave most formidable works. The loss in my regiment was small, only two wounded. The Rebels are now in their works round Atlanta, i. e. "The Last Ditch," and the fighting will no doubt be desperate, but I think Atlanta will fall, and that will end a campaign unparalled in history, where the locomotive and telegraph have followed an invading army to within gunshot of the enemy's lines.

Headquarters 111th Penn'a Vet. Vol.,<br>Near Atlanta, Ga., July 17th, 1864.

DEAR BROTHER:

I am pleased to hear that you have a prospect of getting a situation with a better salary than you had before, and I hope you may be more successful in getting your pay than I was. I will try to get you a still better situation as soon as I can get time to do anything else but fighting. We heard that the Rebels were near Baltimore and also in Pennsylvania. There is some talk of our corps being sent to drive them out, but I do not believe the report. I only wish they would send me there. The raid will enable the Copperheads of Pennsylvania to see what manner of men their Southern friends are. They will undoubtedly give all their friends along their line of march abundant opportunities to display their hospitality. I have no fears for Pennsylvania. Another Gettysburg can and will be fought if necessary. The Johnnies will fail to accomplish their object, which is undoubtedly to draw off a portion of Grant's army. The reported defeat of Hooker's Corps, some time since, is not true. It has never been defeated or repulsed yet. I have taken part in every fight it has been engaged in, and I ought to know. I was in the assault on Kenesaw Mountain, and our corps took and held the position it was ordered to take. Sherman did not, however, accomplish all he expected to accomplish, namely, to drive over 85,000 men from a strongly intrenched position, on an almost inaccessible mountain, but the movement compelled the enemy to leave it during the night. I do not see the object of such false statements being published. The movements of this army have been very successful so far. I have just received orders to move immediately, so must close. I am quite well. Please remember me to all at home, and with kind regards to yourself and family, believe me, ever

Your affectionate brother,<br>
Geo. A. Cobham, Jr.

This was the last letter received from Col. Cobham by any member of his family, and I am dependent on the kindness of many of his comrades for the account of his death, which differ very materially. I accept what I believe the most trustworthy, from an old friend of us both, who was also present at the time and so closely connected with the Colonel that he had better opportunity of knowing the actual state of things.

It seems that the Rebel Gen. Johnson was superceded in command by Gen. Hood, whose first movement was aggressive. On the 20th of July Hood marched out with his whole force in dense column to attack our line, in the center of which was an unoccupied space. When the movement was discovered an order came to Col. Cobham, who was commanding the 3d Brigade, to send a trusty regiment to complete the line, and immediately another, send the 111th Pennsylvania, which he led himself, and reached the point simultaneously with the enemy, and in the encounter, in which the Rebels were repulsed, the Colonel received his death wound from some sharpshooter of the enemy. He was borne to the rear by his comrades, and his last words were, "How Goes it With the Boys," and was satisfied with the news of victory.

"In the beauty of the lilies Christ was born across the sea,
With a glory in His bosom that transfigures you and me;
As He died to make men holy, let us die to make men free,
While God is marching on."

### FROM THE 111TH REGIMENT.
[Warren Mail.]

We conclude to publish only so much of the long letter from the 111th Regiment as is of a nature personal to the regiment or its officers, because the main facts have already been anticipated by the newspaper reports from the army. In describing the taking of a battery or temporary fort on the march toward Resaca, the writer says:

At 5 o'clock P. M. Col. Cobham received a written order from Gen. Hooker to take command of the troops immediately in front of the Rebel works, comprising parts of the 1st, 2d and 3d Brigades of the 2d Division, 20th Army Corps, and if possible obtain possession of the guns and remove them from the fort. Immediately afterwards he was notified that Col. Ireland was wounded, when the command of the 3d Brigade also fell upon him by seniority. He immediately turned over the command of the 111th to Lieut. Col. Walker, and proceeded to execute the order by detailing 50 men without arms, under Lieut. Col. Kirkpatrick, 5th Ohio, to dig down the front of the fort under cover of sharpshooters; after about three hours severe labor amidst a perfect shower of balls from the Rebel breastworks, the guns were drawn out and removed to division headquarters. Too much praise cannot be accorded to the officers and men engaged in this novel undertaking, for the prompt action and coolness displayed under a most severe fire. Capt. Woeltge, Co. I, was killed, and Capt. Wells, Co. F, severely wounded, at the very mouth of the Rebel guns.

\* \* \* \* \* \*

June 6th, march through the town of Ackworth and encamp at Big Shanty, near Lost Mountain. Col. Ireland having recovered from the effects of his wound received at the battle of Resaca, relieves Col. Cobham, who again assumes command of the 111th, having gained fresh laurels and added, if it be possible, to the high estimation in which he is held as a brigade commander. The reputation our brigade, and particularly the 111th, has acquired for bravery and coolness in action, can be attributed to the confidence of both officers and men in the abilities of Col. Cobham and Lieut. Col. Walker as commanders.

\* \* \* \* \* \*

The letter closes by saying:

Among the numerous instances of personal valor displayed by the officers and men of this regiment, (want of space alone preventing the possibility of giving them in detail), special mention is due Captains Warner, Alexander and Blodgett for the manner in which they performed the ardous and dangerous duties assigned them, being together with their comrades detailed on the skirmish line in nearly every engagement and were specially noticed in the official reports. The regiment was also highly complimented by Gen. Hooker for their gallant conduct at the battle of Resaca. G. W.

[The following was published in the Warren *Mail* shortly after the death of Col. Cobham, and was also copied and printed in the Retanstall, (Eng.) *News*]:

### BRIGADIER GENERAL GEORGE A. COBHAM.

Though foreign born, he was an American in all his stern, strong nature—in his love of that Union, Freedom and National Republicanism for which he sacrificed his life.

When once in the service, Colonel Cobham rose rapidly in position and respect, and became distinguished for courage, fidelity and practical usefulness. The furious but fruitless assault on the fortified heights of Fredericksburg—the terrible struggle at Chancellorsville —the masterly beating back of the Rebel invasion at

Gettysburg—the storming of Lookout Mountain, where, as commander of a brigade, he led the advance in that matchless and memorable "battle above the clouds"—and the triumphant advance and series of battles from Chattanooga to Atlanta—all these show him to have been a worthy descendant of any race, and conclusively attest his lofty courage in the hour of danger, his patriotic fidelity to the Union cause and the land of his adoption, and his inflexible purpose to discharge the duties of a citizen and soldier as a brave man should.

We have seldom known a man more unselfish. Despising the petty arts by which so many officers become distinguished on paper, he never allowed his doings to be gazetted by army correspondents. Duty was his guiding star; to it he bent all the powers of a strong body and a stronger will. This took him into the service. This kept him where danger was thickest, attending to the details of the march and the battle, and performing much of the hard work for which others got credit. Knowing no fear, he sometimes exposed himself unnecessarily, and more than once narrowly escaped in former battles.

In the first year of the war, when men were rallying in this country and looking for a leader, he came to us and said, with a sort of religious earnestness which gave us a new idea of the man: "The government must have defenders—the rebellion must be put down with a strong hand—somebody must lead these men—if other and better men do not, I will try." And he did try; and he did succeed. Though unknown beyond his own neighborhood, he infused his own zeal into the hundreds who answered his call. Consolidating these with part of a regiment at Erie, he went in as Lieutenant Colonel and subsequently became Colonel. For a year or so he commanded a brigade, was strongly recommended by Gens. Hooker, Meade, Geary and others for a Brigadier General's commission, and would have received it long ago had he been willing to push his own just claims to promotion.

In person Colonel George Cobham was tall, muscular and commanding. In his manners he was gentlemanly, unpretending and always easy. In his affections he was as true, confiding and unsuspicious as a child. Always sober, dignified and serious, he knew little of the vices and frivolites of the camp or society, and was too faithful to his high ideal of life to stoop to them. Always polite, the humblest citizen or soldier received from him the same respectful consideration as an officer of the highest rank. Hence he was the idol of his men and respected by every officer who didn't shirk his duty. Having great firmness, he never faltered and generally excelled in whatever he undertook. In short, he was one of those earnest, unpretending, true, high-minded men, whom we rarely meet. The service and the world would be better with more such men and such soldiers in it.

As illustrative of his devotion to the old flag and his love for the regiment, we quote his respone to a toast at a public dinner given him by the citizens of Warren, when he was at home on a brief visit last winter. It is a model of its kind, and speaks volumes for his volor and his worth.

Col. Cobham was loudly called for and arose amid a perfect storm of applause. After silence was restored, he said: "Mr. President and Gentlemen—I appreciate the honor of the occasion and am grateful for the kindness you have shown me. I recognize in this not only a compliment to my own services, but a just tribute to the bravery of the boys whom I have the honor to command. The 111th Regiment have left their blood on nearly every battle field since they were organized. They have endured long marches without a murmur, have faced the enemy again and again without a sign of fear, and stand to-day with a line of bristling bayonets, which is a barrier to Rebel occupation in East Tennessee. The army are determined that the rebebellion shall be put down. (Applause.) I helped to plant the flag on the rugged top of Lookout Mountain, and if God spares my life I will help to make it float from the Potomac to the Gulf. (Great applause.) I will carry back to the boys in the field the report of this reception, and there is not one but will clench his musket with a firmer grasp and vow never to lay it down again until the rebellion is crushed. (Applause.) I again thank you for the honor conferred upon me. I have no words to express my gratitude."

Alas! that he was not spared to see and enjoy the full measure of his faith and his ambition. The bravest and best die soonest. God knows what is best in this sore affliction for our national sin; and while we weep for the early lost, let us learn to emulate their virtues and trust in Him who doeth all things well."

## TRUTH VINDICATED.

### A Just and True Statement in Correction of the Official Records, by Capt. James M. Wells.

On July 8, 1863, twenty-five years ago, in the city of Frederick, Md., Colonel George A. Cobham, Jr., then commanding the 2d Brigade, 2d Division, 12th Army Corps and myself held an earnest conversation. Standing in front of me, his hands clasping mine, his lips quivering with emotion, he said to me: "Captain, this is hard to bear. That no wrong may possibly be done, however, I shall be silent." I answered: "Colonel Cobham, the truth shall be made known." To this he answered: "Not now. At the end of twenty-five years, if either or both of us be then living, let the truth be made known." I promised to obey his wish, and we moved on with the moving column in pursuit of Lee and his beaten army. The time has come for me to keep my promise then and there given.

A few days after the disastrous battle of Chancellorsville, Va., fought May 1, 2 and 3, 1863, and lost through the incompetency of General O. O. Howard,

Commander of the 11th Army Corps, Colonel George A. Cobham, 111th Pa. Vols., assumed command of the 2d Brigade, 2d Division, 12th Army Corps, Brigadier Generll Thomas L. Kane, as previous commander, having gone home sick on an indefinite leave of absence. Colonel Cobham commanded the Brigade from then, May 9, 1863, to 6 o'clock a. m., July 2, 1863. At that hour, just as the head of the brigade column was turning to the right from the Baltimore pike to take the position assigned to it on Culp's Hill, Brig. Gen. Kane rode into our midst in an ambulance of the 2d Army Corps and took command of the brigade. Colonel Cobham immediately assumed command of his own regiment, the 111th Pa. Vols. Within a few minutes thereafter, while the brigade was still in motion toward the position assigned to it, Lieut. Col. Thomas J. Leiper, of General Kane's staff, came to Colonel Cobham and, in my presence, delivered an order from General Kane for him, Colonel Cobham, to resume command of the 2d Brigade, as he, General Kane, was too unwell to continue in command. Colonel Cobham went to General Kane for further explanation and received from him in my presence, a second order to resume command of the brigade. Thus ordered, Colonel Cobham turned over the command of his regiment, the 111th Pa. Vols., to Lieut. Col. Thomas M. Walker, and resumed command of his brigade. He lead it forward to the position assigned to it in line of battle, conducted the work of the brigade in the construction of breastworks, commanded and personally superintended every movement of the brigade from a few minutes after 6 o'clock a. m., July 2, 1863, to the close of the battle of Gettysburg. Every order issued to the regimental commanders of the brigade during the battle was given by him. Every change in the line of battle of the brigade was made by his order and under his personal supervision. The fighting of the brigade was done under his eye, under his leadership, in his presence. Its prowess on the field was due to his masterly arrangement of the brigade line, to his personal supervision of every detail in the movements of the troops, to his inspiring and steadying presence among the men. The character of the fighting done by the brigade, under his leadership at that battle, is attested by the punishment inflicted upon the enemy, by their repeated repulses, their overthrow and rout.

General Kane remained with the brigade during the battle, sitting near Colonel Cobham most of the time. He did not command the brigade, he did not issue an order during the battle, he took no part in the movement of the troops, he in no way influenced the fighting of the brigade, he was simply an on-looker.

July 4, 1863, was spent by the members of the 2d Brigade, under orders from Col. Cobham in the burial of the Union and the Rebel dead thickly strewing the field. On July 5 the brigade, under the command of Colonel Cobham, moved from Culp's Hill, where it had done its duty under *his* leadership, marched to Littlestown, Pa.,

and encamped.  On July 6, Brigadier General Thomas
L. Kane wrote and submitted the following report:

> Headquarters 2d Brig., 2d Div., 12th A. C. }
> Near Littlestown, Pa., July 6, 1863. }

CAPTAIN:

I respectfully enclose two of the special reports ordered of the commanders of regiments of my brigade. The report of the 111th Regiment Pa. Vols. has not yet been received. I assumed command at 6 a. m. on the morning of the 2d inst., communication with the army having been cut off so completely by Stuart's cavalry that I succeeded with great difficulty in making my way through to their lines in citizen's dress.

I have to express my thanks to Colonel Cobham, 111th Pa. Vols., who commanded the brigade in my absence, for the high state of efficiency in which I found it. I have recommended this most deserving officer for promotion. The brigade was ordered forward into line with the rest of the division soon after my arrival, and before sundown threw up a substantial breastwork as directed upon the excellent position assigned them. At twilight we were removed to the batteries on the turnpike and shortly after ordered to return to our former position. On entering the wood, within two hundred paces of our breastwork, we were met by a sharp fire, which we supposed to come from the First Brigade, misled by the darkness. The men were, therefore, ordered not to reply, but withdraw to the turnpike and marched in by another road. We moved directly to the position of the 3d Brigade (where the noble Greene, by his resistance against overwhelming odds, it should be remembered, saved the army), and making our way past Greene's right, were again fired upon. thus discovering that the enemy had entire possession of our works. Their front was then opposite Greene's right flank, he holding them there. There was nothing to be done but to connect with Greene, fold down to the right along the best ground offering, and strengthen the right flank as much as possible. The attack in force upon us commenced at 3:30 a. m. July 3d. The Confederate Major General Johnson's division led, followed by Rhodes'. The statement by our prisoners is that they advanced in three lines, but they appeared to us only as closed in mass. We ceased firing occasionally for a minute or two to induce the enemy to come out of advantageous positions, where they paid for their temerity, but with this exception kept up a fire of unintermitting strength for seven hours, until about 10:30 o'clock, when the enemy made their last determined effort by charging in column of regiments. Their advance was Stuart's brigade of Johnson's division. The 1st Maryland Battalion (Confederate States) left most of their dead in line with our own. It can not be denied that they behaved courageously. Our own loss was 23 killed and 73 wounded. Twenty men have been missing since we were fired on in the woods on Thursday night. After this repulse the enemy fell back, and, although they kept up a desultory fire for some time after, it was plain, as the result proved, that the battte was over.

By the accompanying report of Lieut. W. H. White, Co. G. 29th Pa. Vols., you will see that the number of Enfield rifles left by the enemy on an area of about two acres in front of our second position was 1803. The reports of burying parties will probably show that not less than 500 men were left dead there. The whole number of men of my brigade who were in this action was 632. They justified their reputation as marksmen. I have not the name of a single straggler or recreant reported to me. Every officer and man of my command did his duty, and I must on this account, refuse myself the privilege of naming particular any of the numerous examples of heroism which I witnessed. I should acknowledge the valuable services of Lieuts. Thomas J. Leiper and J. Spencer Smith, of my staff. In the absence of Capt. J. P. Green, Asst. Adjt. Gen., Lieut. Leiper served as acting Asst. Adjt. Gen. with unvarying ability.

The few we had killed were unhappily among our best men. Second Lieut. Edward J. Harvey, Co. K, 29th Pa. Vols., was a man of fine mind and elevated character. Lieut. McKeever, Co. A, 29th Pa. Vols., an ardent patriot and faithful officer; Sergeant Major Charles H. Lefford, 29th Pa. Vols., a youth of the fairest promise; Color Sergeant John E. Greenwood, 109th; Sergeants E. F. Allen, 111th, and Anthony E. Thomas, Edward M. Summercamp and Jacob Lower, 29th; Corporal Louder, 29th; and Privates John Sherman, Moreland Campbell, Charles

Miller, John M. Richardson, 111th; Casper H. Warner, Thos. Acton, Robert Hews, Robert Luckhart, John Applegate, John Watson, Emanuel McLaughlin; James Morrow, 29th; Thomas Ocks and Delancey Veale, 109th; were all patriotic and brave men, whose loss is seriously to be deplored. Young Veale, often noticed for his singularly handsome and bright countenance, was Adjutant's clerk of his regiment, but insisted on going into action with his rifle.

Very respectfully your obedient servant,
THOMAS L. KANE,
Brigadier U. S. Volunteers.

CAPT. THOMAS H. ELLIOTT,
Assistant Adjutant General.

The conversation July 8, 1863, between myself and Colonel Cobham, was in regard to the foregoing report. I asked him whether he had finished his report of the part taken by his brigade in the battle of Gettysburg. He answered that he had made no report, that Brig. Gen'l Thomas L. Kane had taken that honor upon himself and had made a report. Realizing the position in which he had been placed by the action of General Kane, keenly alive to what that action brought to him, he spoke as I have written, and added: *"Captain Wells, having commanded this brigade throughout the greatest and most important battle in the annals of the world, I shall not be known in history as having been a participant in the battle. Lieut. Col. Walker reports the part taken in the battle by the 111th Pa. Vols., and Brig. Gen'l Thomas L. Kane reports the part enacted by this brigade. Where am I? Where shall I appear? I certainly fought at Gettysburg."* The pathos of these words as they fell from his quivering lips can not be expressed. Other words were spoken by him, personal to myself, which have no place here. The wrong done him, however, unwittingly it may have been, was to be in part repaired, and in a way of which he then had no knowledge. On August 12, 1863, a circular order was issued by the commander of the army, Major General George C. Meade, in compliance with which, Colonel Cobham on August 15, 1863, wrote and submitted the following report:

> Headquarters 2d Brig., 2d Div., 12th A. C.
> Near Ellis' Ford, Rappahannock River,
> August 15, 1863.

CAPTAIN:

In compliance with circular order from Headquarters Army of the Potomac, August 12th, 1863, I have the honor to submit the following report of the movements of the brigade from June 28 to July 26:

At 4 o'clock on the morning of June 29 the brigade broke camp about one mile from Frederick City, Md., marching through Frederick, Walkersville, Woodsborough, Pipeville and Brueville, and encamped for the night, having marched 20 miles. On the 30th, marched to Littlestown, Pa., 15 miles. July 1, marched by the Baltimore turnpike to Two Taverns, and from there to within about two miles from Gettysburg, when the brigade was placed in position, by direction of Brigadier General Geary commanding division, on the crest of a hill overlooking part of the battlefield, and in support of a battery stationed on a hill. Here the troops lay on their arms during the night.

About 6 o'clock on the morning of July 2, Brigadier General Kane arrived on the field in an ambulance of the Second Army Corps, and assumed command of the brigade. I then took command of my own regiment, the 111th Pa. Vols., but in a few minutes General Kane sent me an order by one of his aides, Lieut. Leiper, to resume the command of the brigade. I reported to the General, when he repeated the order to me. I accordingly turned over the command of my regiment to Lieut. Col. Walker and resumed the command, General Kane being too much prostrated to continue it. However, he gallantly remained on the field, although too feeble to resume the arduous duties of his post.

Orders were then received to move forward into line with the rest of the division. An excellent position was chosen for us by General Geary, connecting on the left with the 3d Brigade, on a heavy wooded hill, where we threw up a breastwork of logs, stone and earth, running at right angles to those of the 3d Brigade. The position was a strong one, and admirably located to command the approaches by Rock Creek. Here we remained till evening, when we were ordered to the support of the 3d Corps; but, before marching a mile this order was countermanded, and I was directed to return to our former position. On the head of the column entering the wood, it was fired upon from behind the stone wall in the rear of our breastworks, which the enemy had taken possession of during our absence. Not being certain whether the fire came from the enemy or our own division (it being dark), I withdrew the brigade to the pike and marched further up the road, and entering the woods in the rear of the 3d Brigade, took a position in line nearly at a right angle with our breastworks, sheltered in a great part of the line by a ledge of rocks, and connecting on the left with the 3d Brigade, thus partially enfilading the enemy's position. The 147th Pa. Vols. of the 1st Brigade, which arrived soon after, took position on our right, which position they resolutely held during the heavy attack next morning. At 3 o'clock next morning, July 3, the enemy's skirmishers commenced firing on us, by 4 o'clock the firing had become general along the whole line on both sides. The regiments relieved one another, one at a time, long enough to replenish their supply of ammunition and wipe out their rifles. The firing was kept up briskly on both sides with but little intermission till about 10 o'clock a. m., when a desperate charge was made on our lines. The enemy advanced in columns, closed in mass, determined to make one last desperate effort to drive us back at the point of the bayonet. They were, however, driven back with heavy loss, and retired in confusion, retiring beyond the line of breastworks.

The brigade was now relieved for a short time by a brigade of the 6th Army Corps. About 2 p. m. the brigade again took possession of the breastworks, relieving the other brigade (Shaler's). Occasional firing was kept up during the night, and by daylight the enemy withdrew from the front of our lines. The 29th, the 109th and the 111th Regiments, Pennsylvania Volunteers, are deserving of much praise for their courage and good conduct during the severe fire to which they were exposed. Col. Rickards, 29 Pa. Vols., Lieut. Col. Walker, 111th Pa. Vol., and Capt. Gimber, 109th, who commanded the regiment, also deserve special mention for their gallant conduct on this occasion. Our loss was 23 killed, 66 wounded and 9 missing. On the 4th the brigade remained on the battlefield; burial parties were sent out with every available pick and shovel to bury the dead. Our own, as well as a large number of the enemy's, were buried, but a very large number of the Rebel dead were left unburied on the field.

On the 5th, left the battlefield and marched to Littlestown, 10 miles.

July 7, left camp, and, marching through Braceville, Pipeville, Woodsborough and Walkersville, encamped for the night; distance 26 miles.

July 8, started at 4:30 a. m., marched through Frederick and Jefferson; distance 18 miles.

July 9, broke camp at 5 a. m. marched to Burkesville, crossed the Blue Ridge at Crampston Gap, encamped at Rohrersville; distance 9 miles.

July 10, started at 5 a. m., marched through Keedysville, and took up position in line on right of the 1st Brigade, near the edge of a piece of woods. July 11, advanced about 3½ miles; took position on the left of line of battle, threw out skirmishers in front and on the left flank.

July 12, changed position about one mile to the right. July 13, about 1 a. m. again changed position half a mile to the right, on a rise of ground near Saint James' College and Marsh Run. Here an excellent and substantial breastwork of rails and earth was constructed under the personal direction and supervision of the General commanding the division. July 14, the brigade remained in the entrenchments ready to support the troops that advanced on the enemy's position at 5 a. m. of this day.

July 15, left entrenchments about 7 a. m., marched through Sharpsburg and past the Antietam Iron Works and encamped near the foot of the Maryland Heights, having marched 17 miles. July 16, left camp at 5 a. m. and marched by way of Harper's Ferry to Pleasant Valley, where we encamped, and remained until the 19th, to obtain necessary clothing and equippage for the troops; distance, 9 miles.

July 19, broke camp at 4 a. m.; crossed the Potomac and the Shenandoah at Harper's Ferry, and marched up London Valley to near Hillsborough, Va., distance, 15 miles. July 20, left at 4:30 a. m.; marched through Woodgrove and Slabtown and encamped near Snicker's

Gap, remaining until the 23d; distance, about 10 miles; broke camp at 5 a. m. marching through Snickersville to Upperville and Paris, relieving a brigade of the Second Army Corps stationed at Ashby's Gap; left at 3:30 p. m. and, marching through Milltown and Forestville, encampdd for the night near Manassas Gap; distance marched, 23 miles.

July 24, marched through Manassas Gap to near Front Royal, and returned and encamped for the night near Piedmont; distance, 18 miles. July 25, left camp at 5:30 a. m. and marched through White Plains to near Thoroughfare Gap and encamped for the night; distance, 16 miles. July 26, marched at 5 a. m. through Thoroughfare Gap, Haymarket, Greenwich and Catlett's Station, and encamped near Warrenton Junction, distance, 22 miles.

The distance marched from June 28 to July 26 was 250½ miles.

Very respectfully your obedient servant,
GEO. A. COBHAM, JR.,
Colonel Commaning 2d Brigade.
CAPT. THOMAS H. ELLIOTT,
A. A. A. G. 2d Div., 12 Army Corps.

Both of the foregoing reports have been taken from the official records of the War Department, Washington, D. C. History, as generally seen and read, records Brigadier General Thomas L. Kane as the commander of the 2d Brigade, 2d Division, 12th Army Corps at the battle of Gettysburg, Pa. Maps of that battlefield portraying the positions of the troops there engaged, place *Kane's* brigade on Culp's Hill. For twenty-five years citizens of this republic, visiting the scene of that momentous and all-important struggle, have had pointed out to them the ground where "Kane's brigade so nobly fought." The name of the hero, Cobham, who *did* command the 2d Brigade, 2d Division, 12th Army Corps July 2 and 3, 1863, on that bloody field, has seldom been spoken by guide or visitor on the spot where, under *his* leadership, *not* Kane's, *Cobham's* brigade bravely stood and fought and won. Hereafter let the good citizens of Warren, Pa., in whose midst repose the remains of Geo. A. Cobham, Jr., know and speak the truth of history here written. They know full well the modest, manly life he led among them from boyhood to mature manhood. Let them also know that, from first to last, in camp and field, he lost none of the graces that won their respect; that in the service of his country, in sunshine and in storm, in the midst of victory or defeat, *everywhere*, he retained his self-respect, was always the courteous, gentleman, a man of upright, stainless life, generous in his judgments, just in deed and word, loyal in his friendships, wise in counsel, guardful of the interests of his men, self-poised, gallant and able in command, in battle supremely brave. As a regimental commander, he had no superior. As commander of brigade, he had few equals. His modest demeanor, his sterling worth, his blameless life, his cool and steadfast courage and his ability were recognized and appreciated by leaders such as the dashing Geary, the heroic Hooker, the matchless warrior, George H. Thomas. These men, whose deeds are historic, whose judgment of men was unerring, knew his merits, esteemed and honored him. In his death, they confessed a loss to the service and to the cause for which he died greatly to be deplored.

The promise I made twenty-five years ago is fulfilled. My duty to my friend is done. In the doing, I find a bounding joy, which only the loyal in heart can feel. His memory, redolent of kindly words, of manly, heroic deeds, I confidently leave in the keeping of my comrades, whom he led and loved, and in whose midst he fell bravely fighting for his flag, and nobly died.

JAMES M. WELLS,
Captain Co. F, 111th Pa. Vols.

www.ingramcontent.com/pod-product-compliance
Lightning Source LLC
Chambersburg PA
CBHW032250080426
42735CB00008B/1082